Beautiful Roses
A Grayscale Coloring Book for Adults

Dar Payment

The Amazing Grayscale Coloring Company
Lake Elsinore, CA USA

Book design and cover art
By Dar Payment

Photographs sourced from Pixabay and PublicDomainPictures.net

Copyright © 2017 by Dar Payment

All rights reserved. No part of this book may be reproduced, stored in a retrieval system or transmitted, in any form or by any means, electronic, mechanical, photocopying, recording or otherwise, without the prior written consent from the author.

ISBN-13: 978-1976548321

Published by:

The Amazing Grayscale Coloring Company
A Division of DAP Publishing
Lake Elsinore, California USA

www.AmazingGrayscale.com

A Note from the Author

It was not my original intention to put together a coloring book. I am not a professional artist, but I love to color grayscale! And to be honest, the grayscale coloring selection I have shared with you in the following pages of this book are from one of my own private collections.

About a year ago I became totally fascinated with every aspect of coloring – especially with projects concerning grayscale. I was so excited that I began to host small coloring parties with my friends, offering many of the grayscale pages appearing in this book for our coloring inspirations.

My friends loved the coloring projects. Soon they were hooked and told me they wanted more similar grayscale pages to color!

These friends would often show their finished coloring projects with their friends, who wanted to color too . . . and well, the rest is joyful providence. The cumulation of the grayscale coloring book you are now holding in your hands.

Have fun bringing the images to life by filling them up with tons of beautiful color. And if you become obsessed with coloring like I did (and still am) and want to spread the love of coloring with your friends too, host your own coloring party using the pages of this book!

Blessings and Happy Coloring,

Dar Payment

"I prefer living in color." ~ David Hockney

How to Color Grayscale

Coloring grayscale is very easy, and there are a few schools of thought out there about how to color a grayscale image or photograph.

The number one thing about coloring grayscale is that the shading is already there for you which means no more trying to figure out where your light source or shadows need to be, etc..

The first grayscale coloring method is to use one color over each area first using very light pressure over the entire area you wish to color. Next, using the same color apply heavier pressure in the darker shaded areas.

Another method is to simply use your darkest colors to color over the areas with the heaviest gray shading. Then your lighter colors over the areas with the lightest gray shading, and finally using your medium colors to blend both the light and dark colors.

The point is that there is no wrong or right way to color grayscale. So have fun experimenting as you unleash your inner colorist, and enjoy watching as your photo or image comes to life before your eyes.

Need samples of coloring inspirations for the images in this book? Download a free full colored template containing all of the coloring inspirations depicted in this book at: https://www.amazinggrayscale.com/Free-Downloads.php

The Best Artist Mediums for This Book

The best artist mediums for this book are colored pencils. You can experiment with gel pens and markers if you'd like, but gel pens and markers will bleed through the page.

If you do choose to use gel pens or markers the best practice is to put a piece of paper underneath your coloring project in order to protect from bleed through onto the coloring page underneath it.

"If I had a rose for every time I thought of you, I'd be picking roses for a lifetime."

~ Swedish Proverb

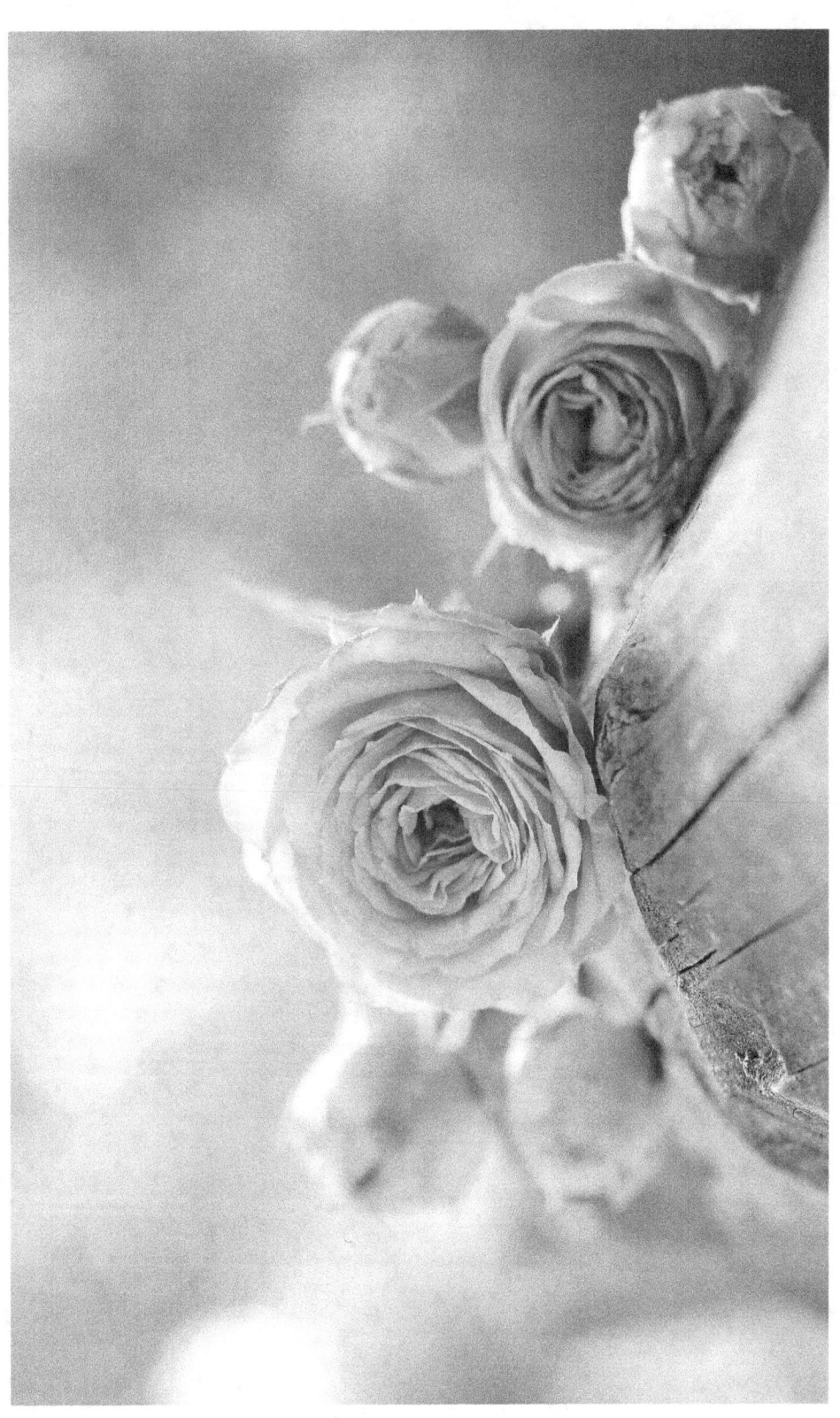

"The rose has thorns only for those who would gather it."
~ Chinese Proverb

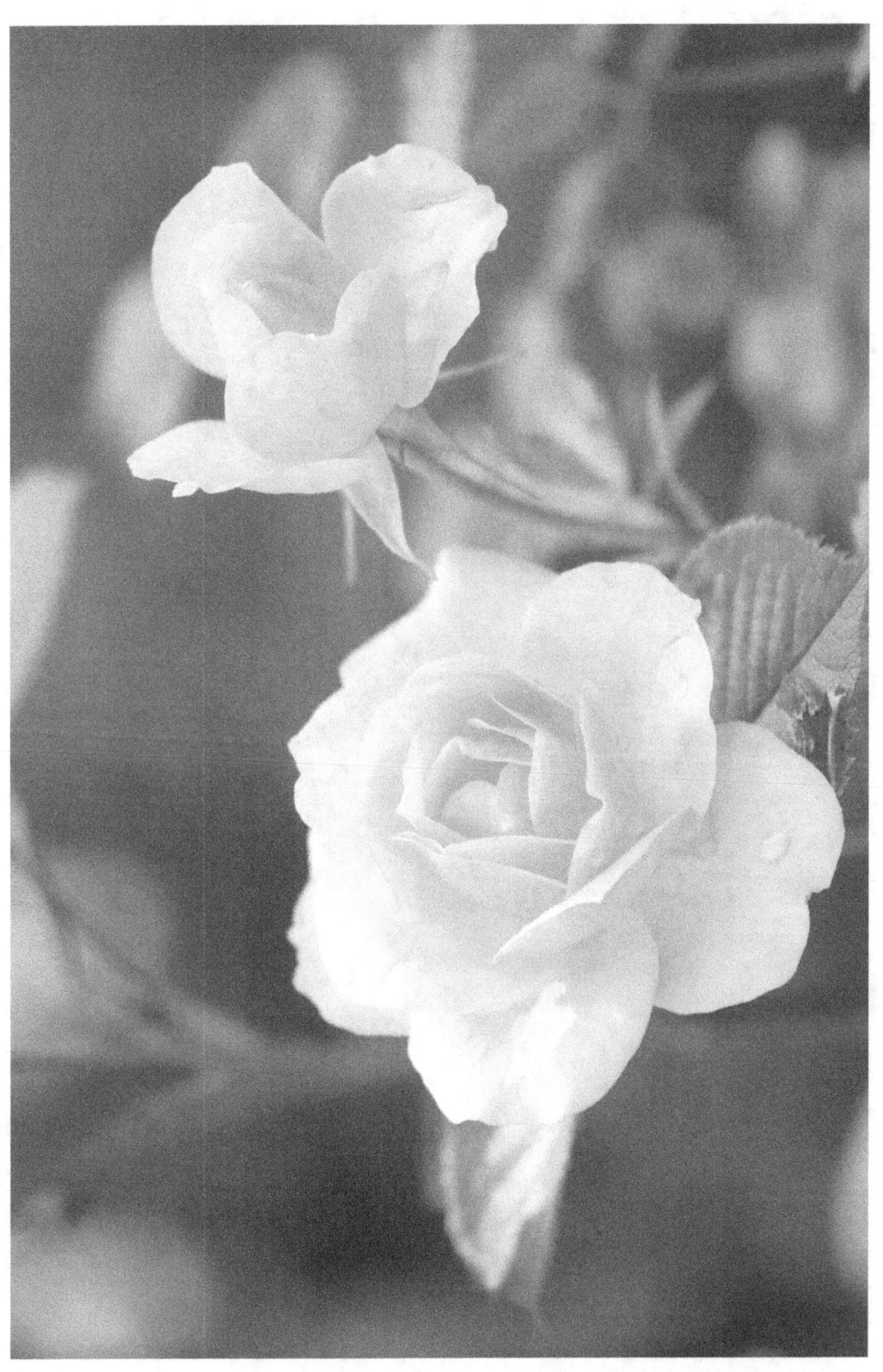

"The Rose is without an explanation;
She blooms, because She blooms."
~ Angelus Silesius

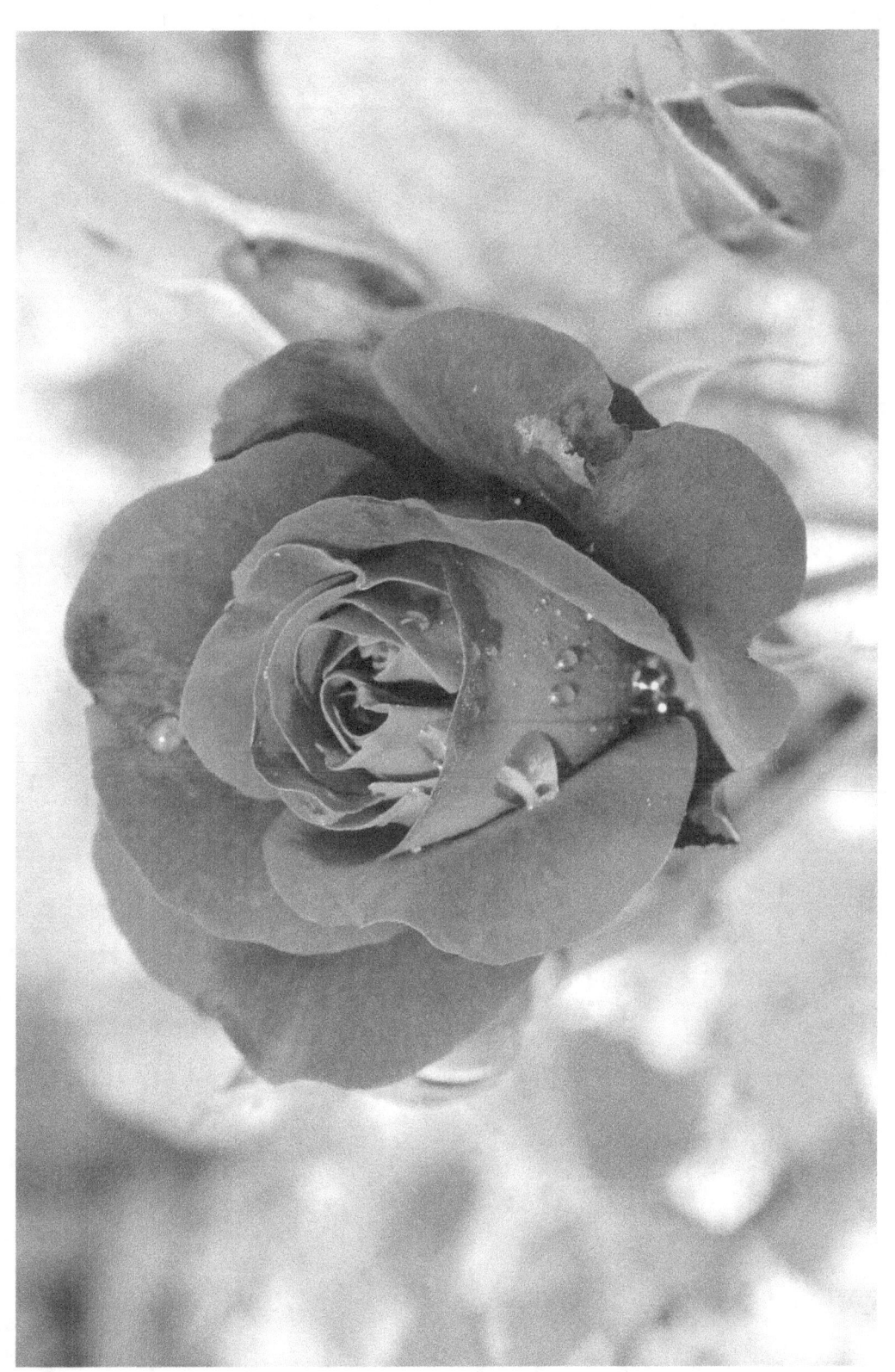

"The rose is a rose from the time it is a seed to the time it dies. Within it, at all times, it contains its whole potential. It seems to be constantly in the process of change: Yet at each state, at each moment, it is perfectly all right as it is."
~ Paulo Coelho

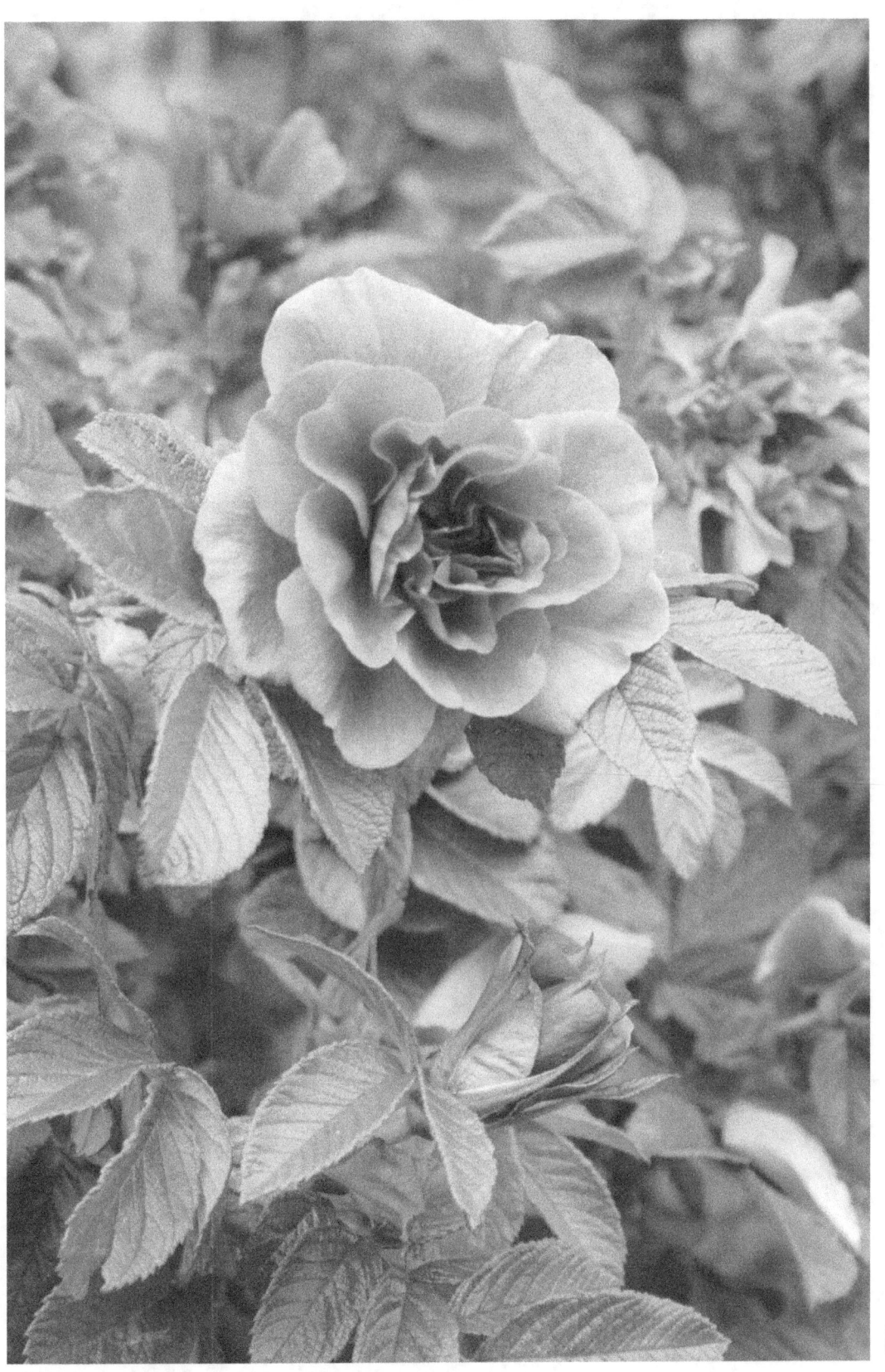

*"There is simply the rose; it
is perfect in every moment of
its existence."
~ Ralph Waldo Emerson*

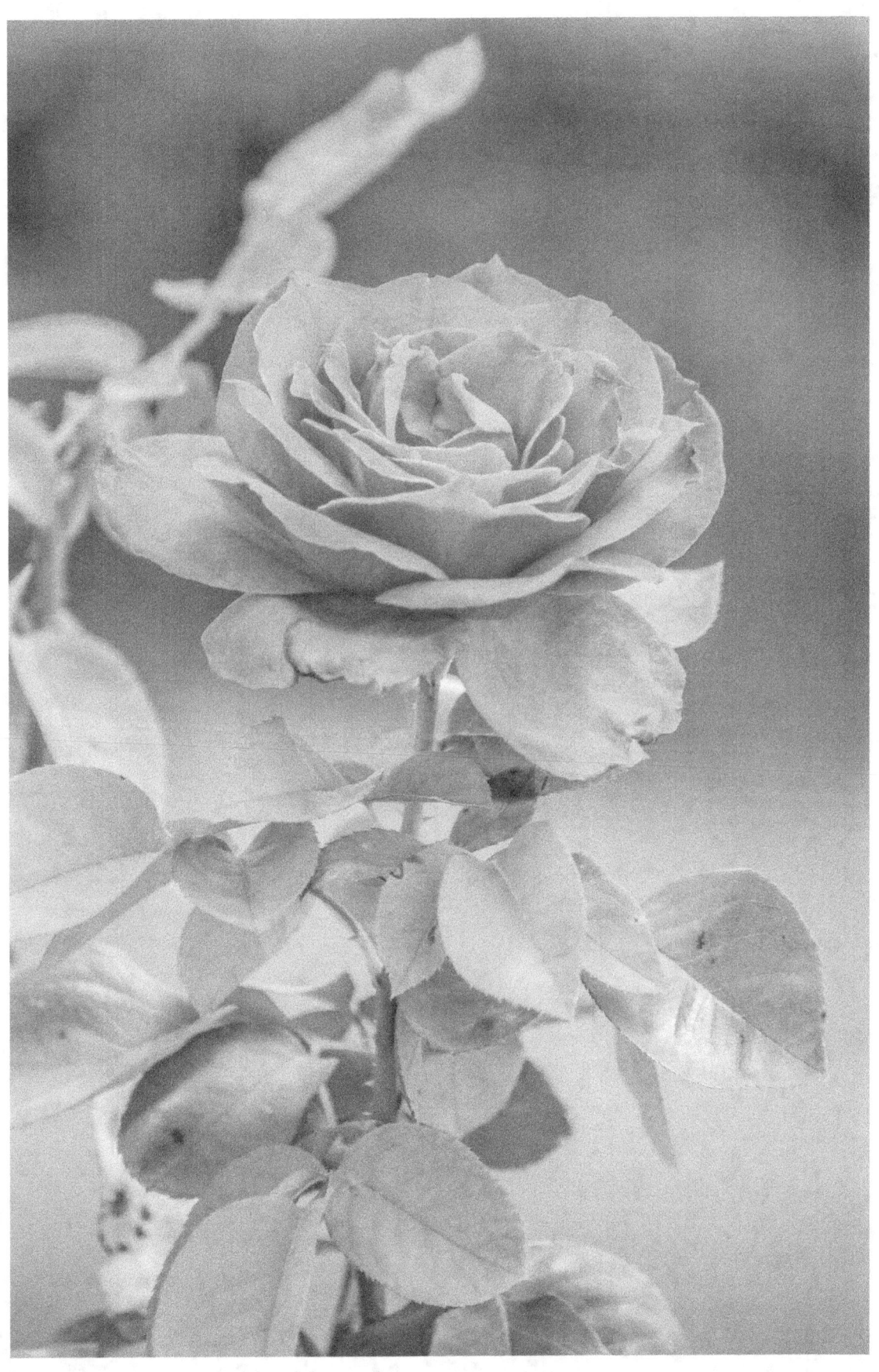

"What a lovely thing a rose is."
~ Arthur Conan Doyle

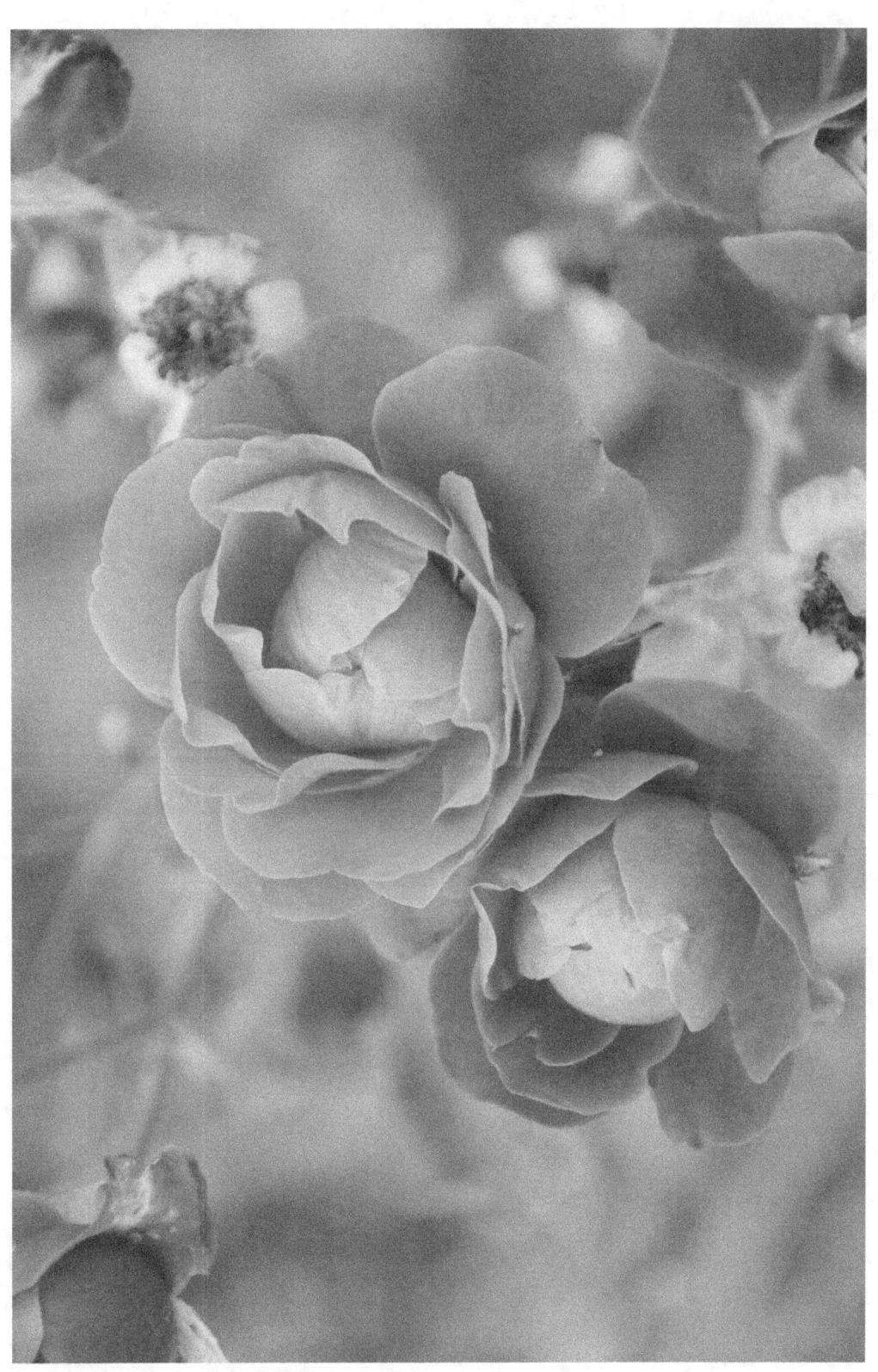

"I'd rather have roses on my table than diamonds on my neck."
~ Emma Goldman

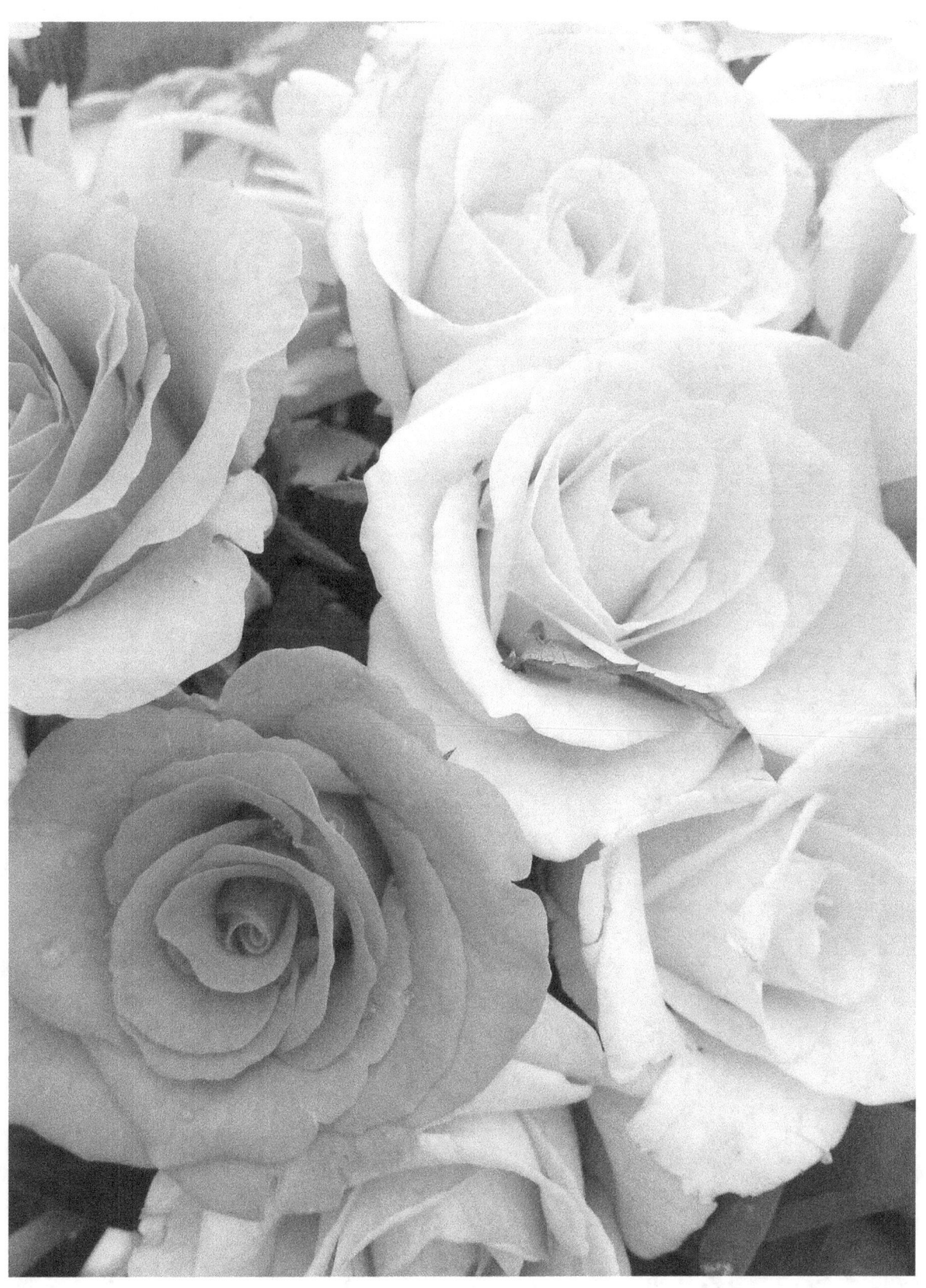

"Which is loveliest in a rose? Its coy beauty when it's budding, or its splendor when it blooms?"
~ George Barlow

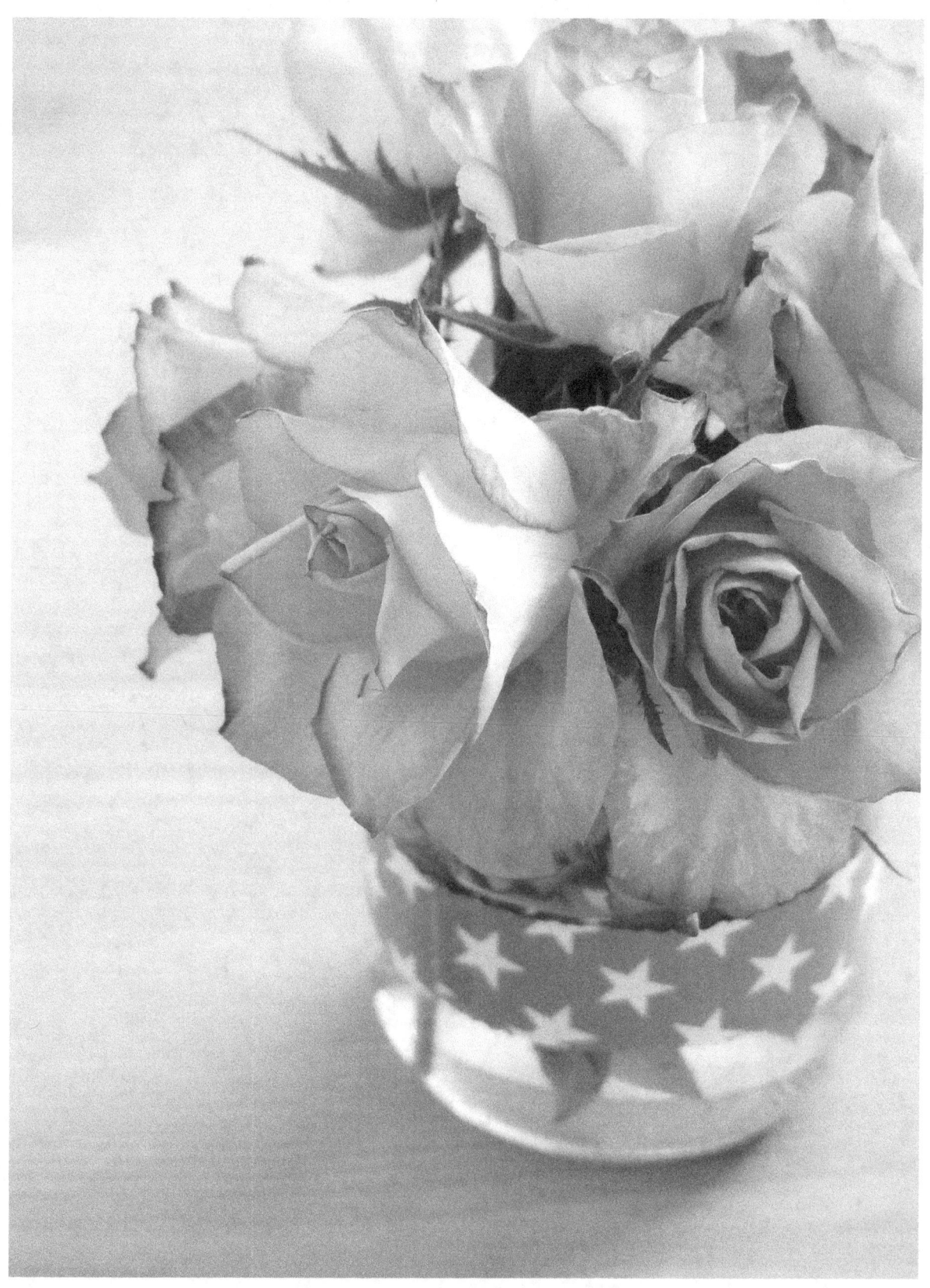

"Rose is a rose is a rose is a rose."
~ Gertrude Stein

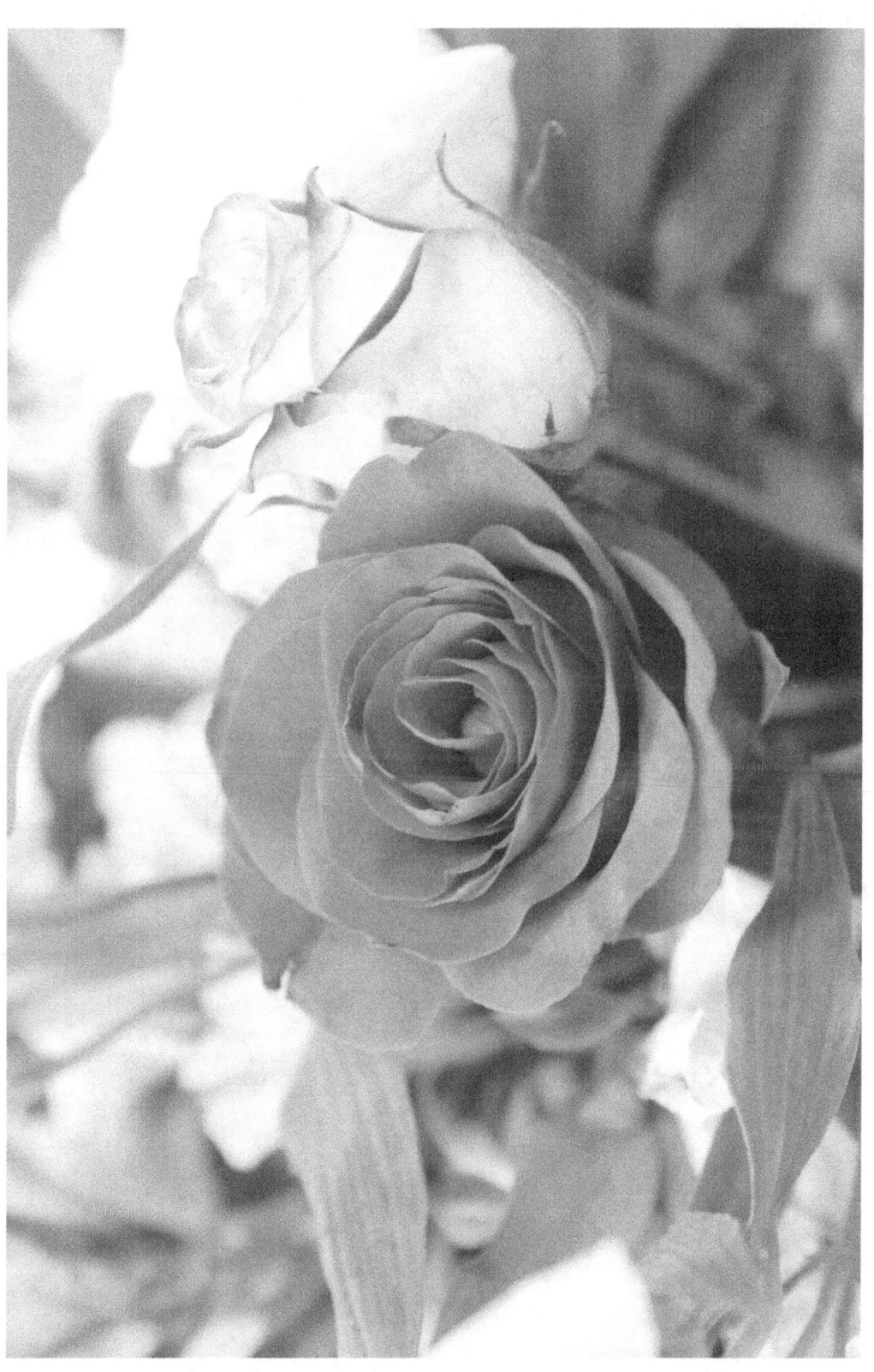

"If the rose is beautiful flower, it is also because it opens itself."
~ Charles DeLeusse

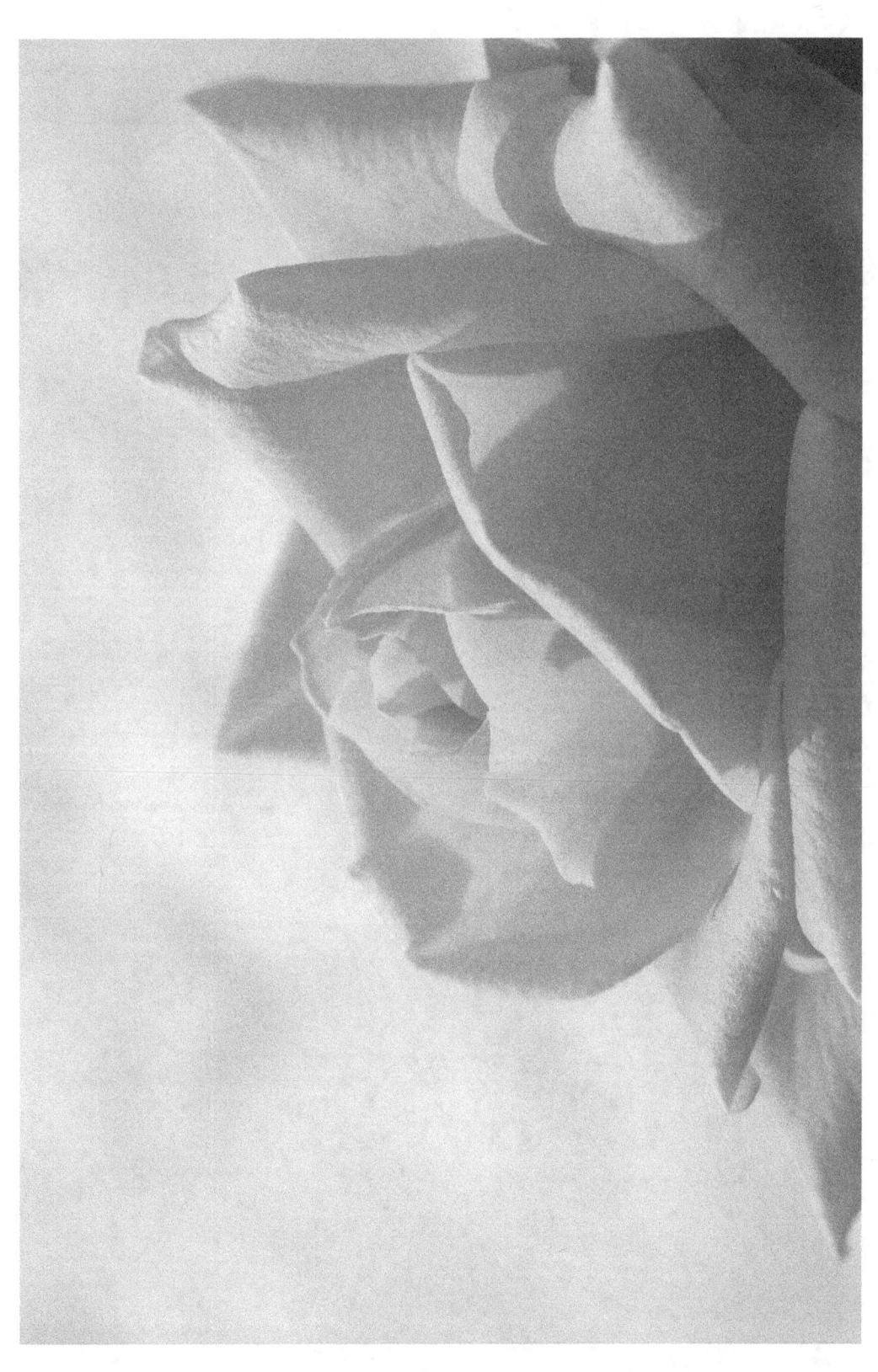

"Where you tend a rose, my lad, a thistle may not grow."
~ Frances Hodgson Burnett

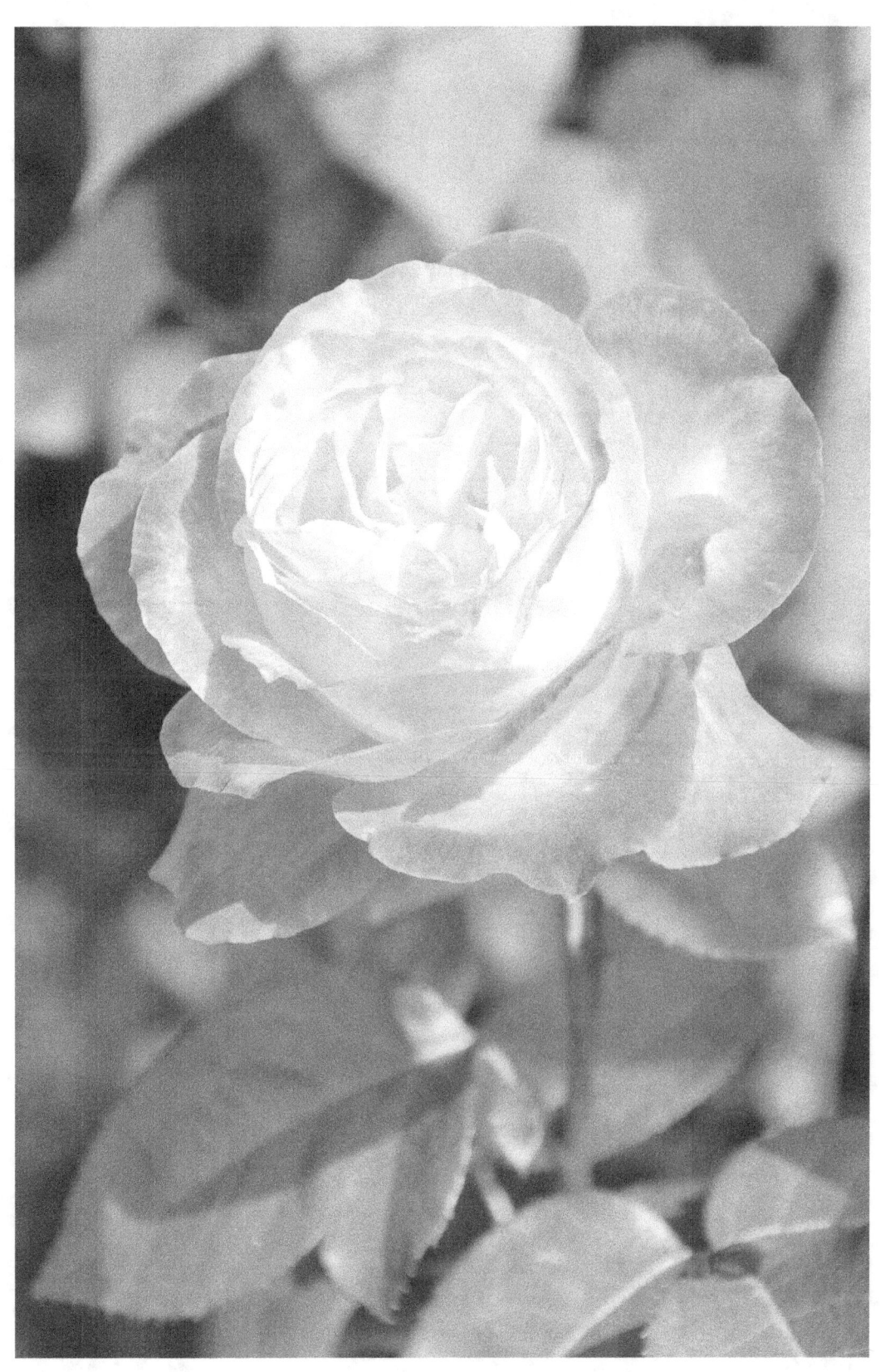

"Gather the rose of love whilst yet is time. ."
~ Edmund Spenser

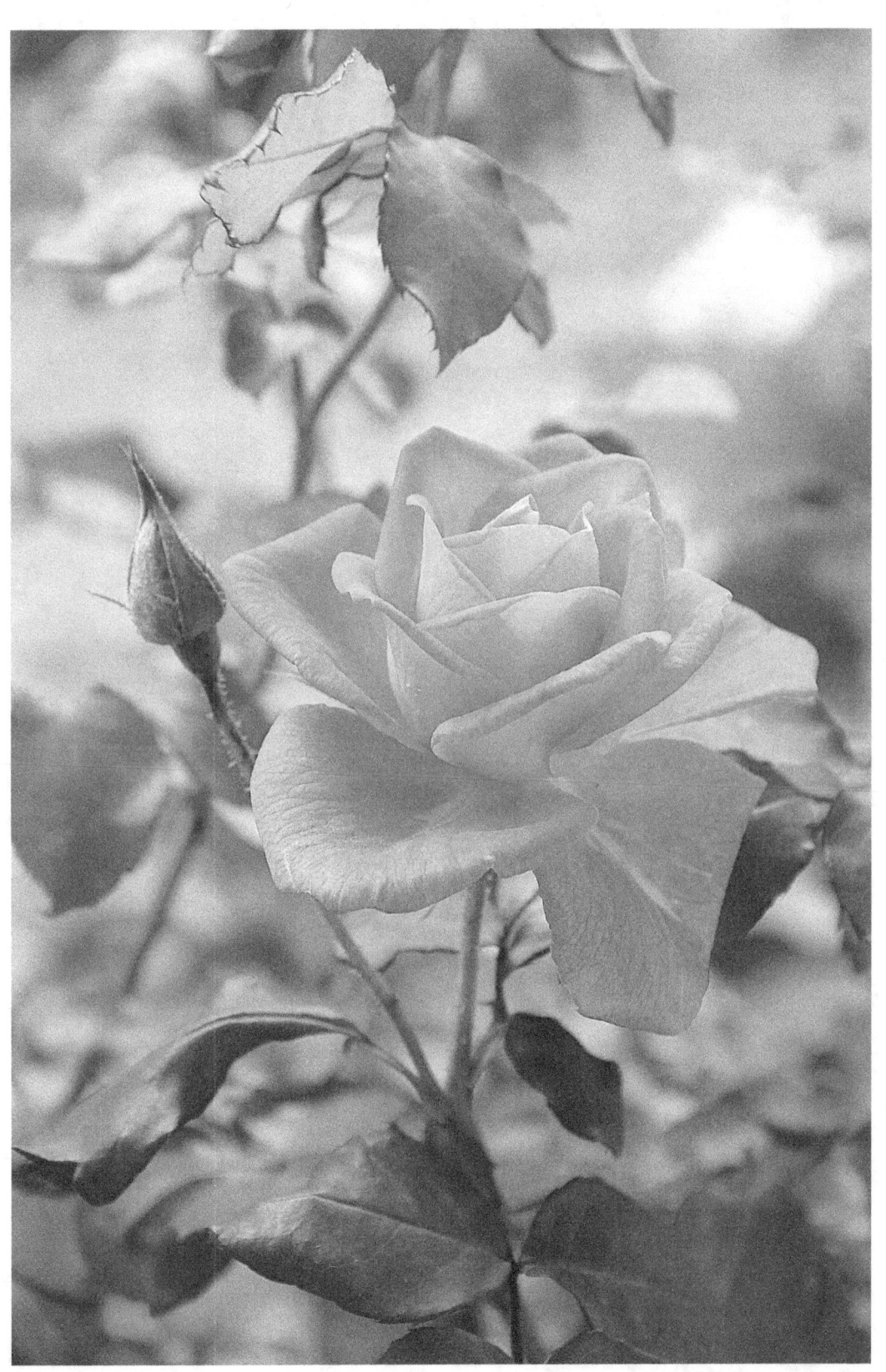

"It is the time you have spent on your rose that makes her so important."
~ Antoine De Saint-Exupery

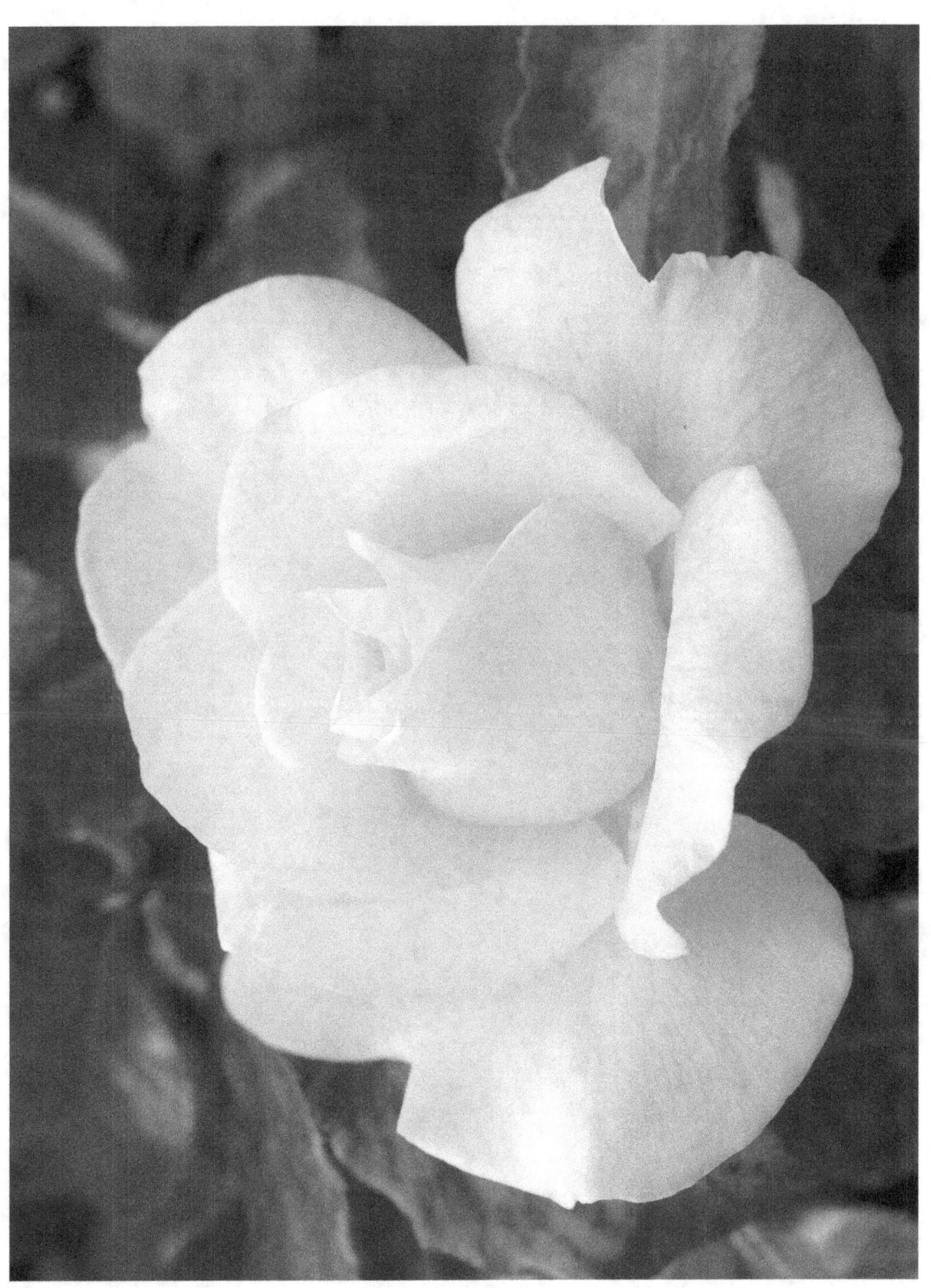

"Take time to smell the roses."
~ Proverb

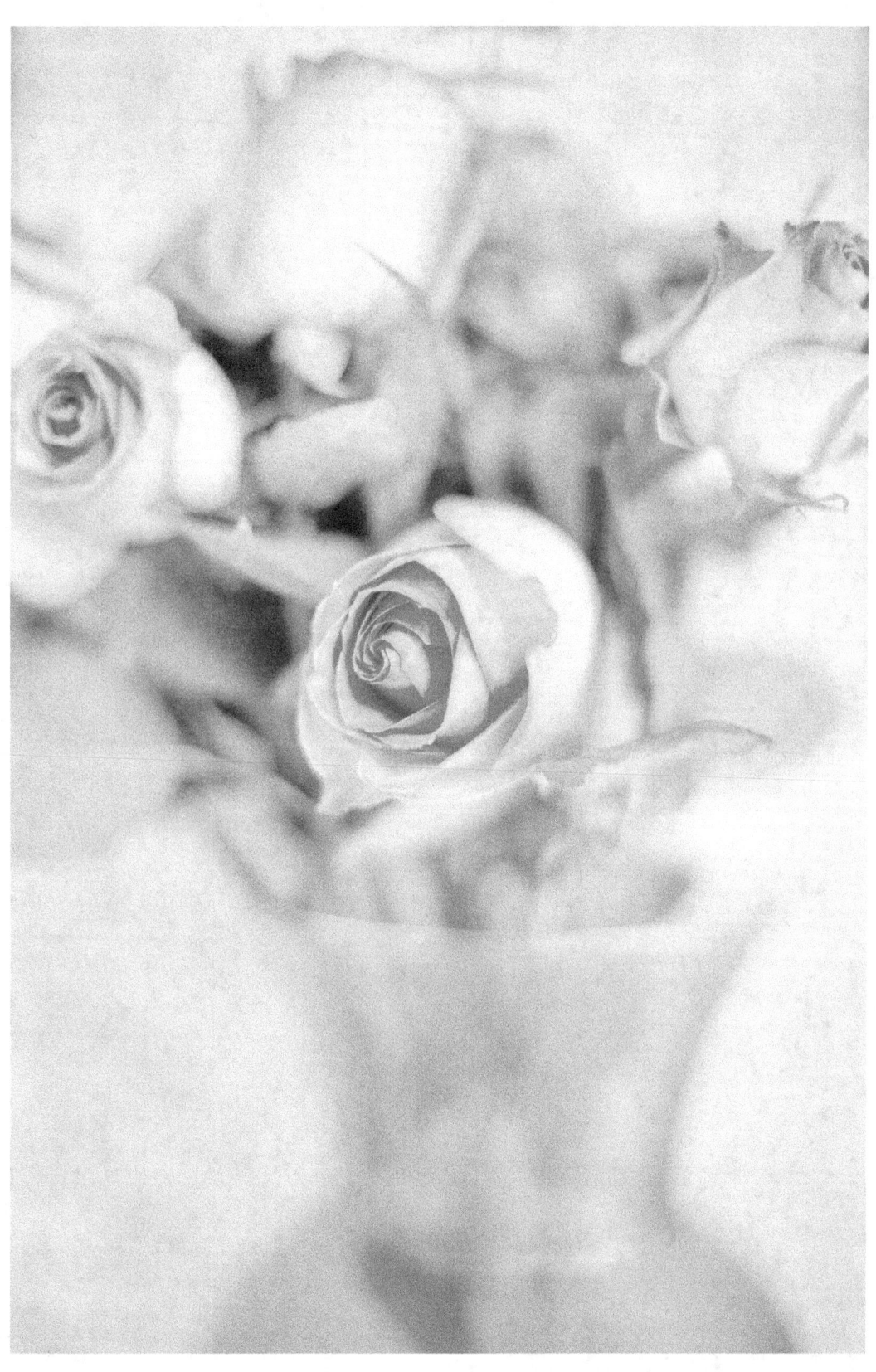

"Love is like a rose. When pressed between two lifetimes, it will last forever."
~ Anonymous

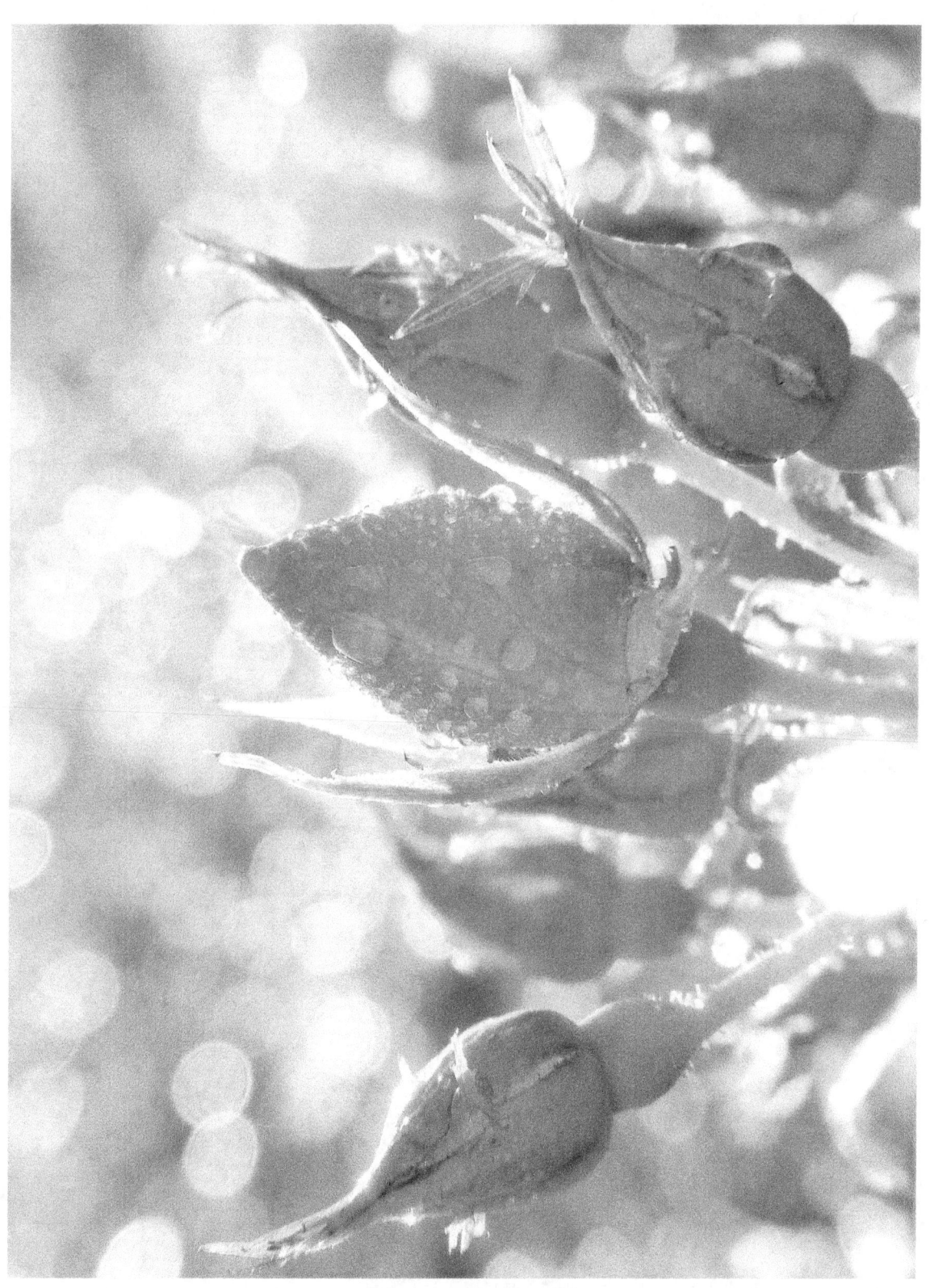

" I don't know whether nice people tend to grow roses or growing roses makes people nice."
~ Roland A. Browne

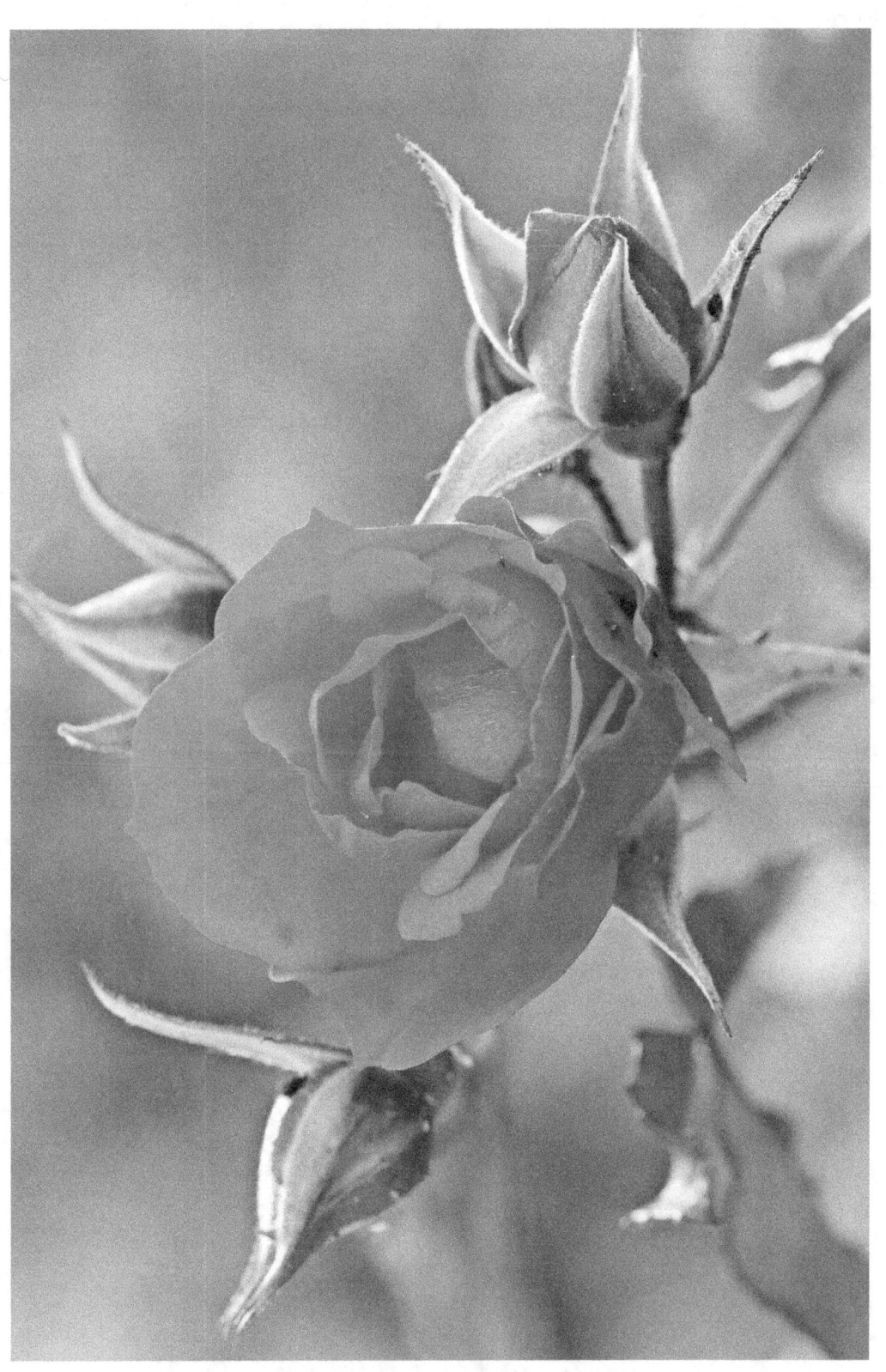

"There may be many flowers in a man's life, but there is only one rose."
~ Unknown

"The rose is a flower of love. The world has acclaimed it for centuries. Pink roses are for love hopeful and expectant. But the red roses, ah the red roses are for love triumphant."
~ Unknown

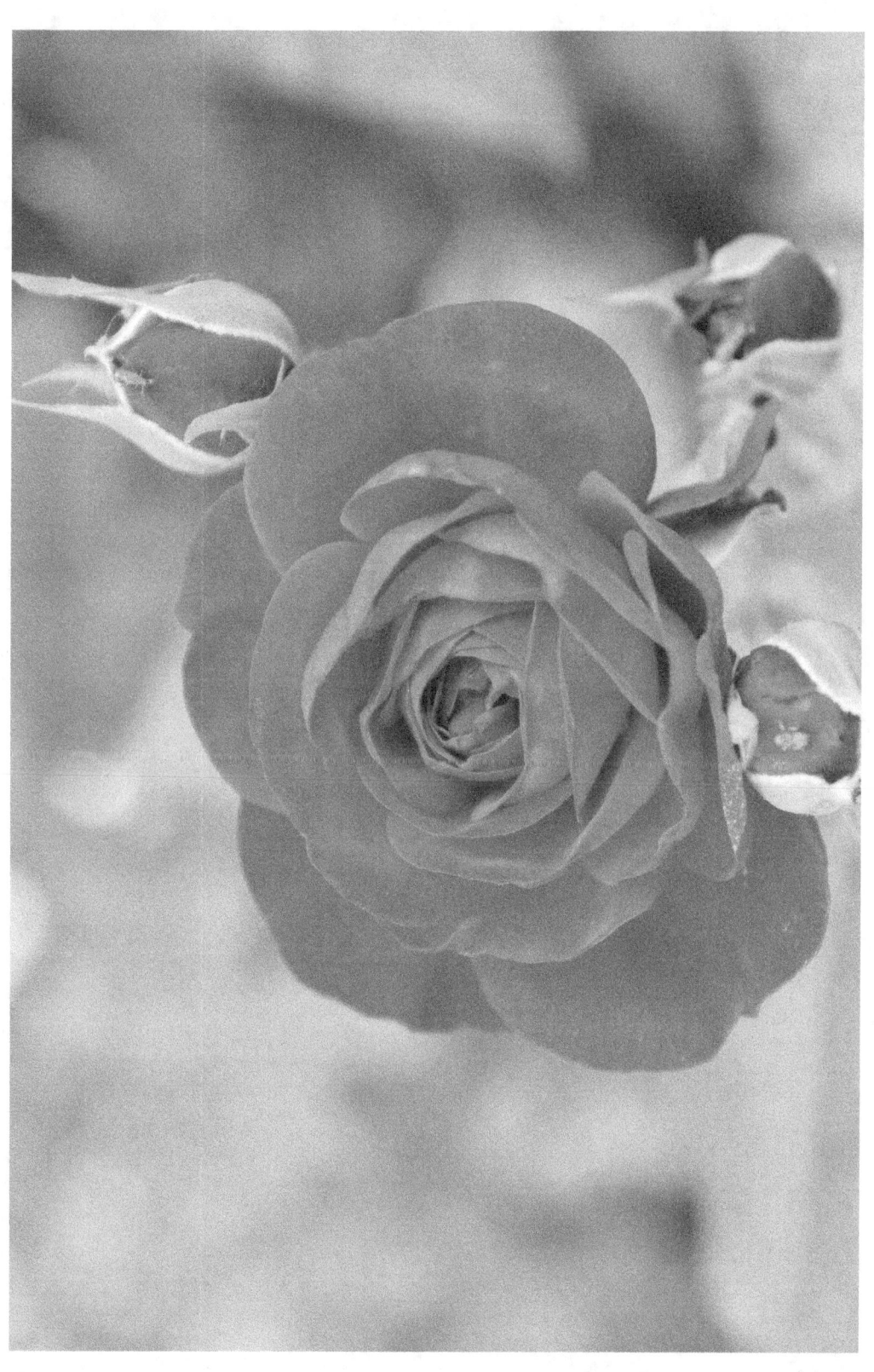

"When I resemble her to thee oh rose, how sweet and fair she seems."
~ Edmund Muller

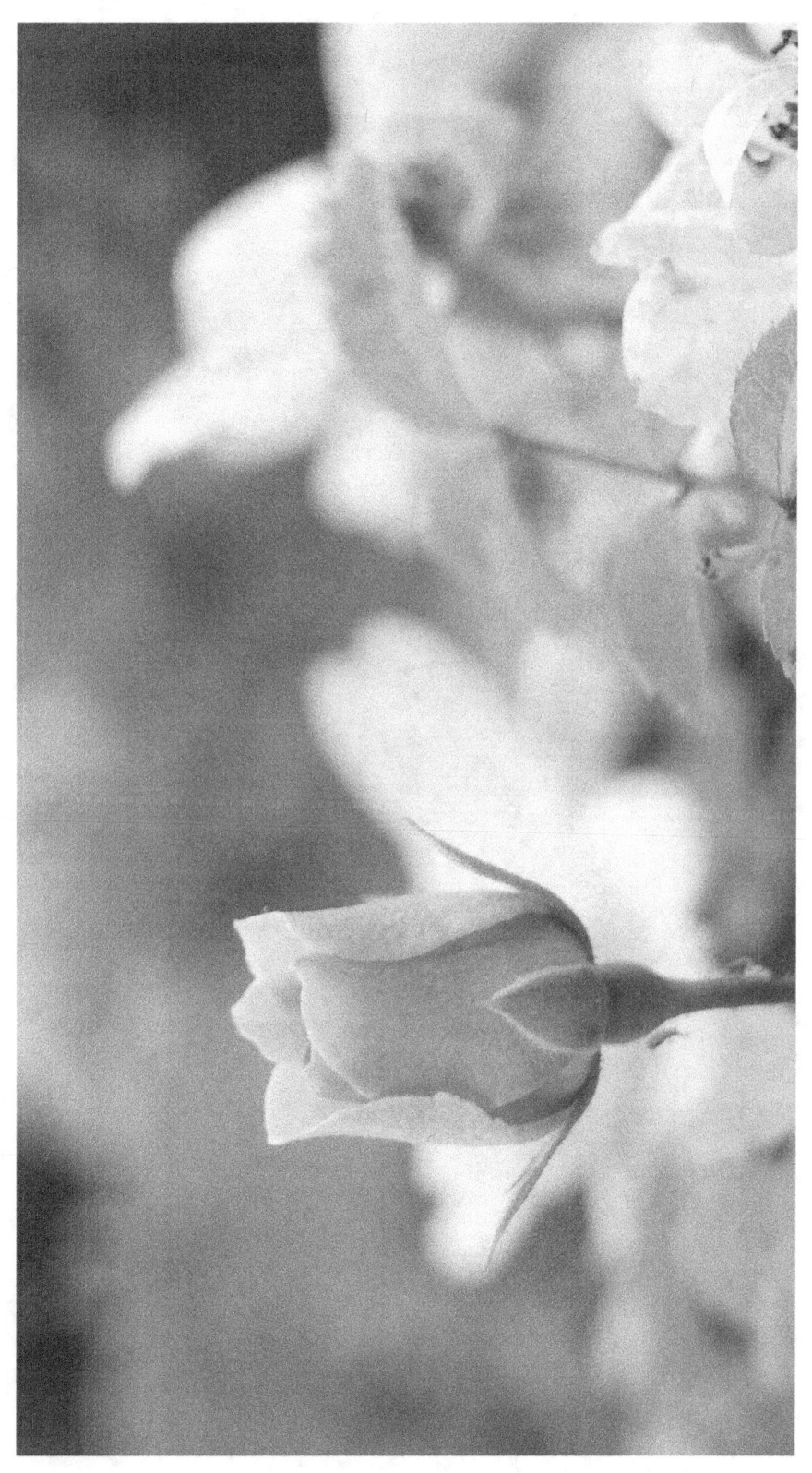

*"Let the beauty and fragrance of a rose
add color to your soul."
~ Illyssa*

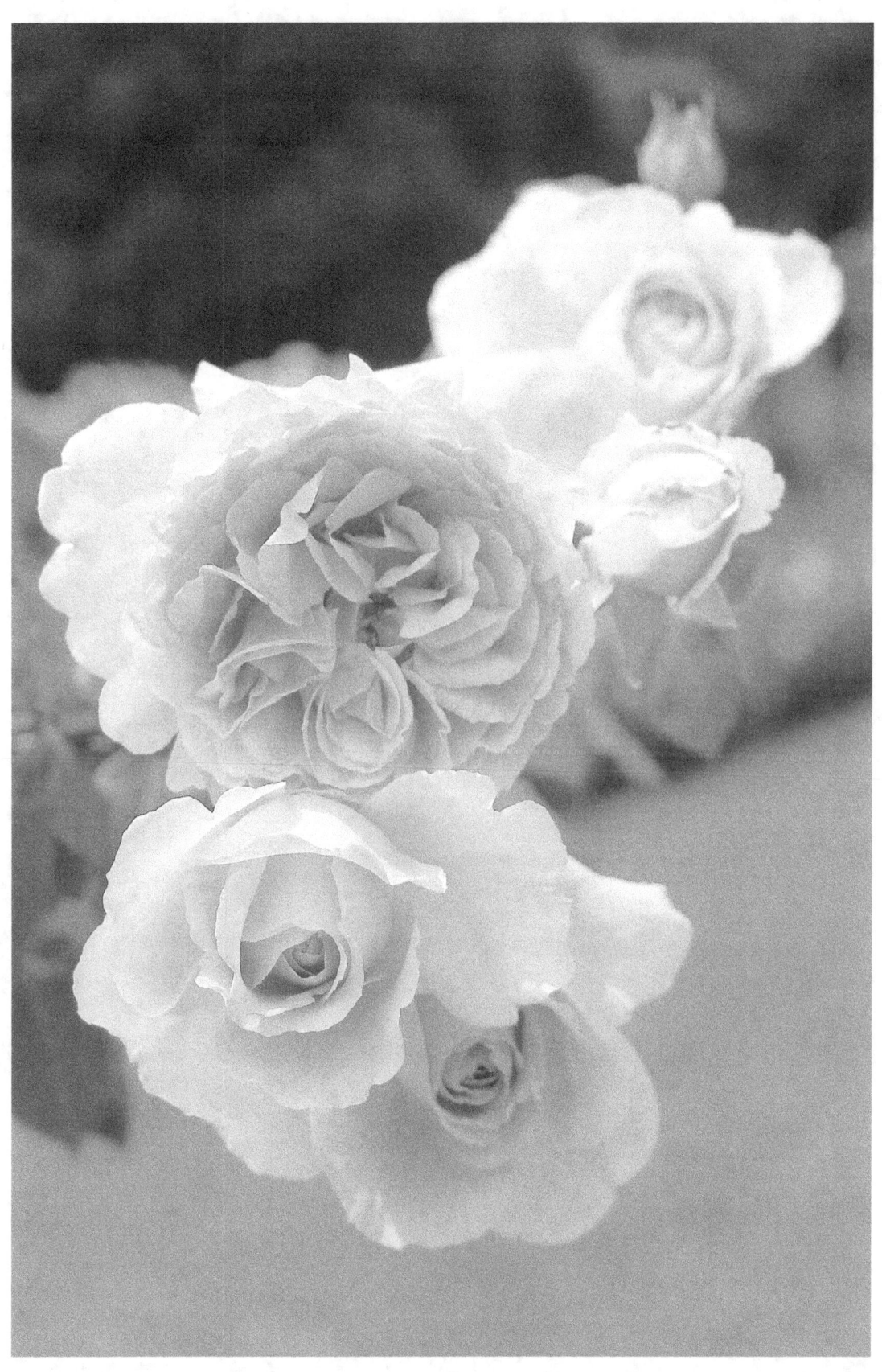

"But friendship is the breathing rose, with sweets in every fold."
~ Oliver Wendell Holmes

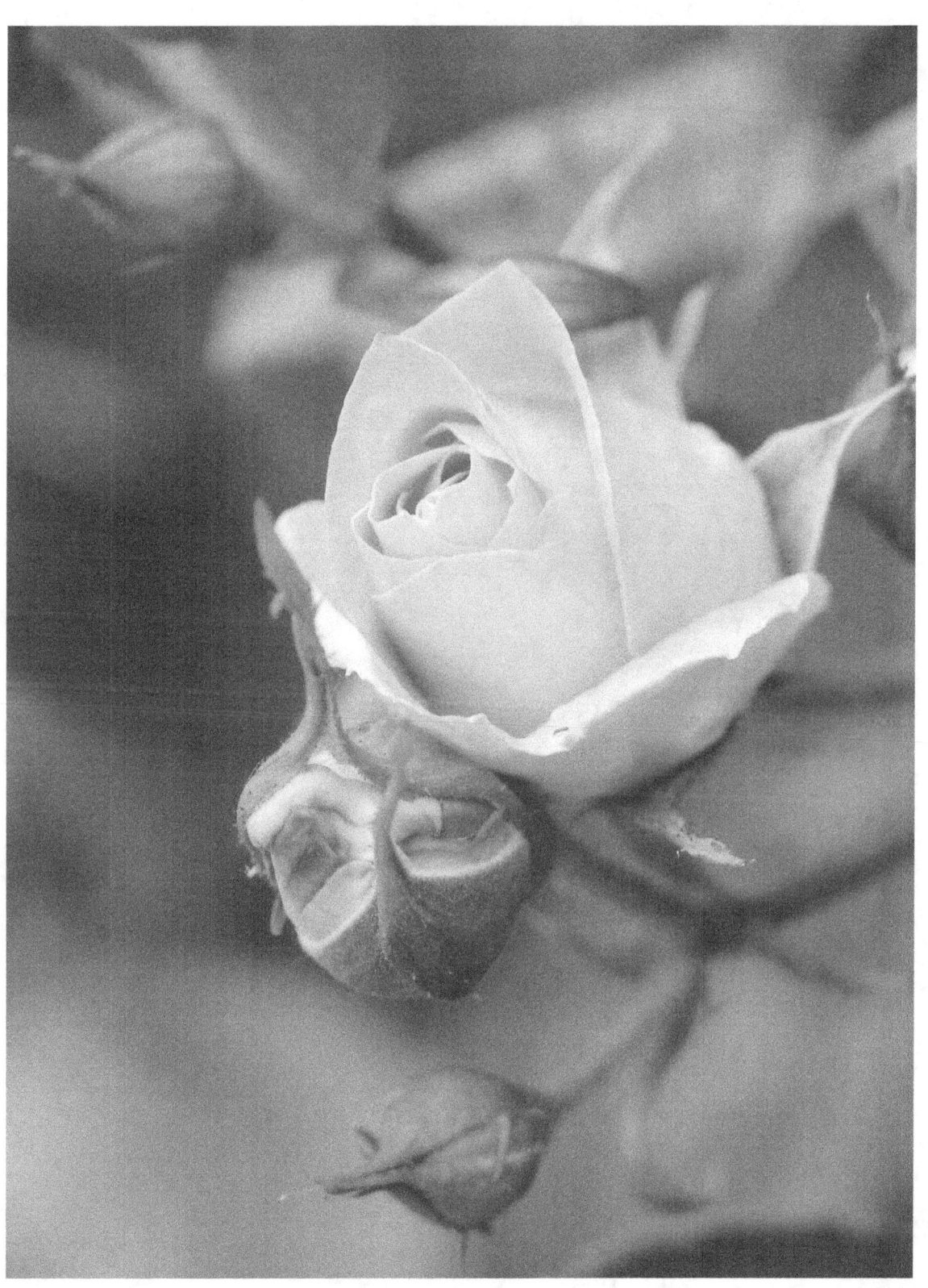

"... a work of art is like a rose. A rose is not beautiful because it is like something else. Neither is a work of art. Roses and works of art are beautiful in themselves."
~ Clive Bell

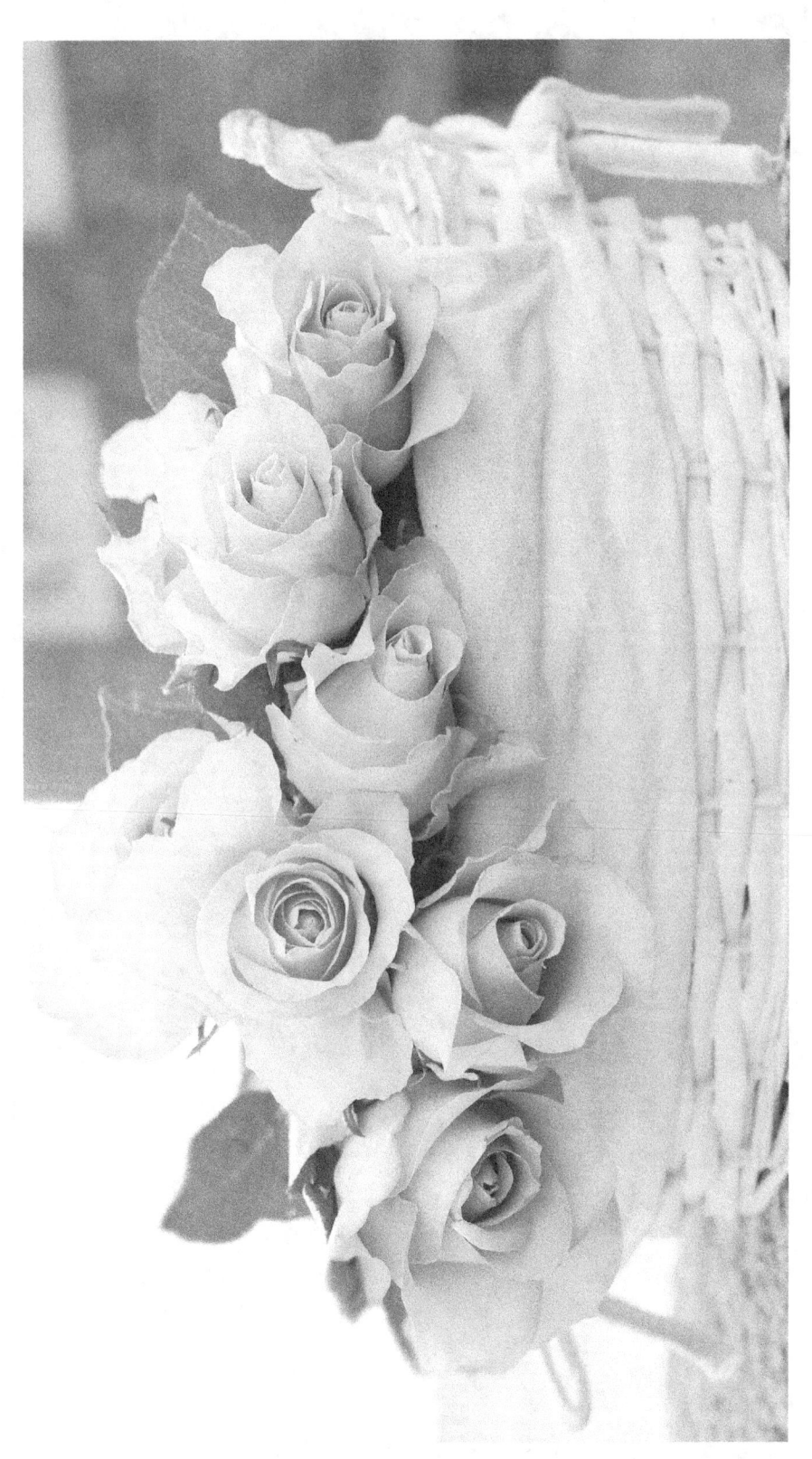

"The optimist sees the rose and not its thorns; the pessimist stares at the thorns, oblivious to the rose."
~ Kahlil Gibran

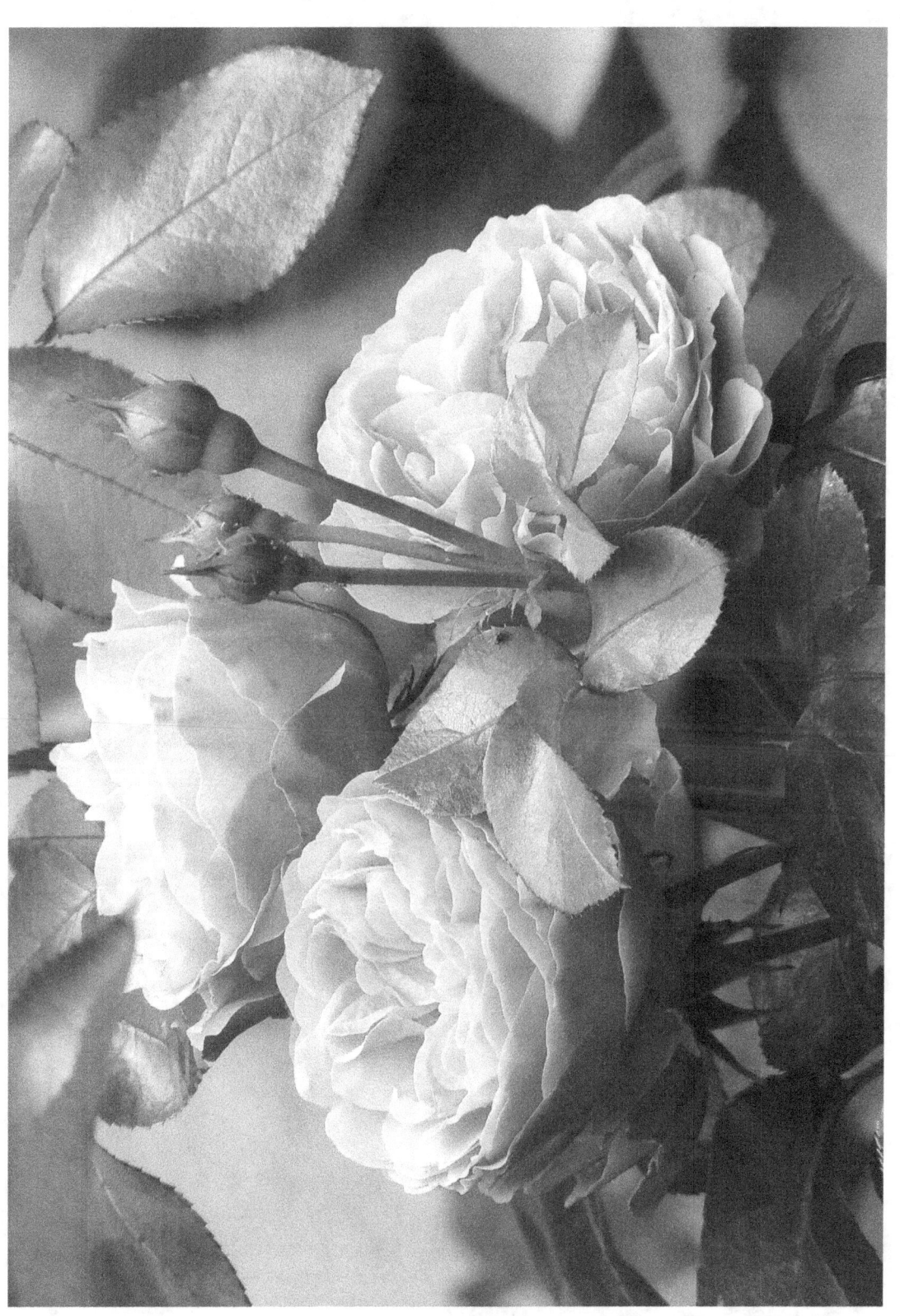

"My love is like a rose divided into two, the leaves I give to others, but the rose I give to you."
~ Unknown

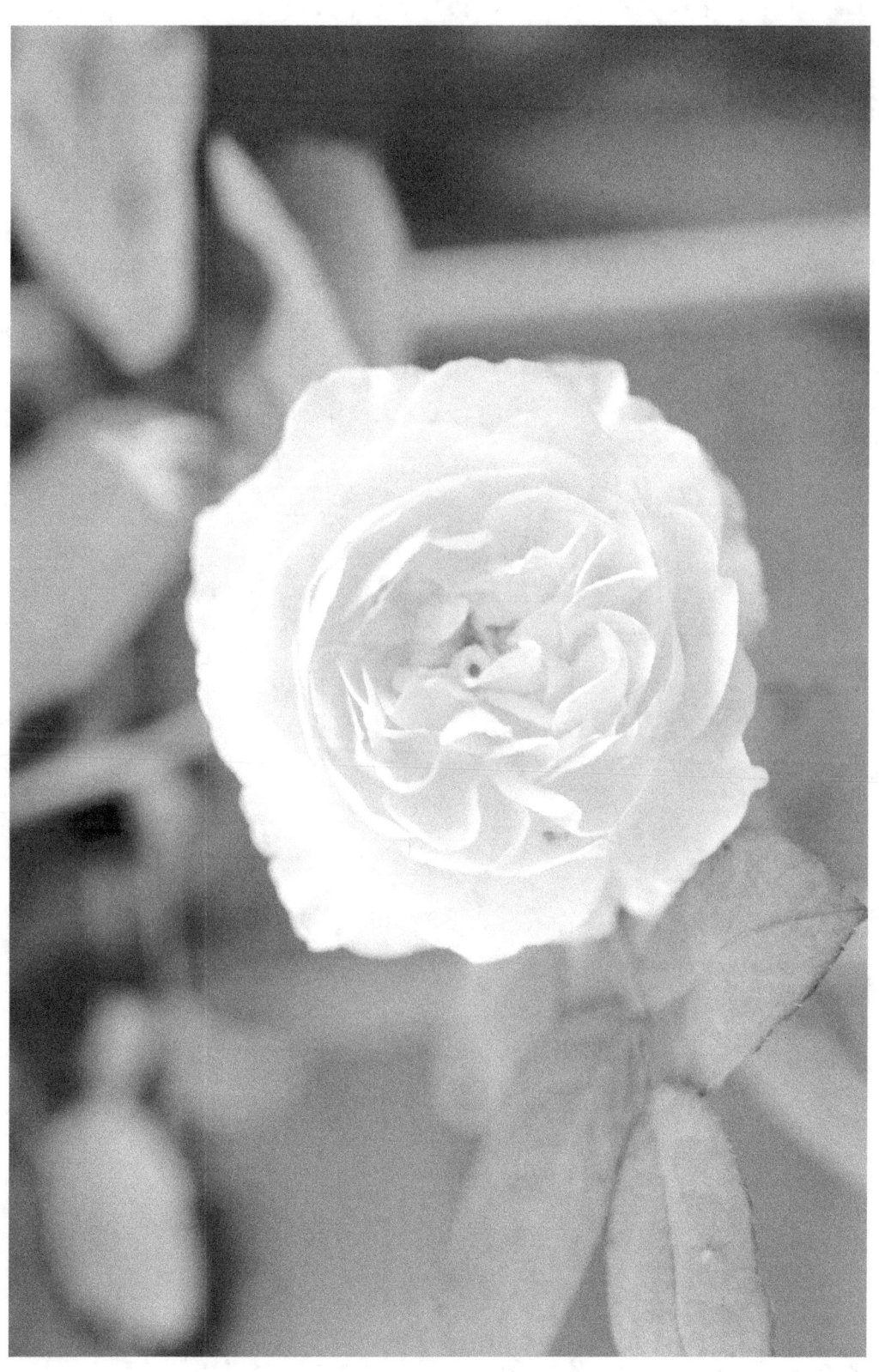

"Just remember, during the winter, far beneath the bitter snow, that there's a seed that with the sun's love in the spring becomes a rose."
~ Amanda McBroom, Songwriter,
The Rose, 1979

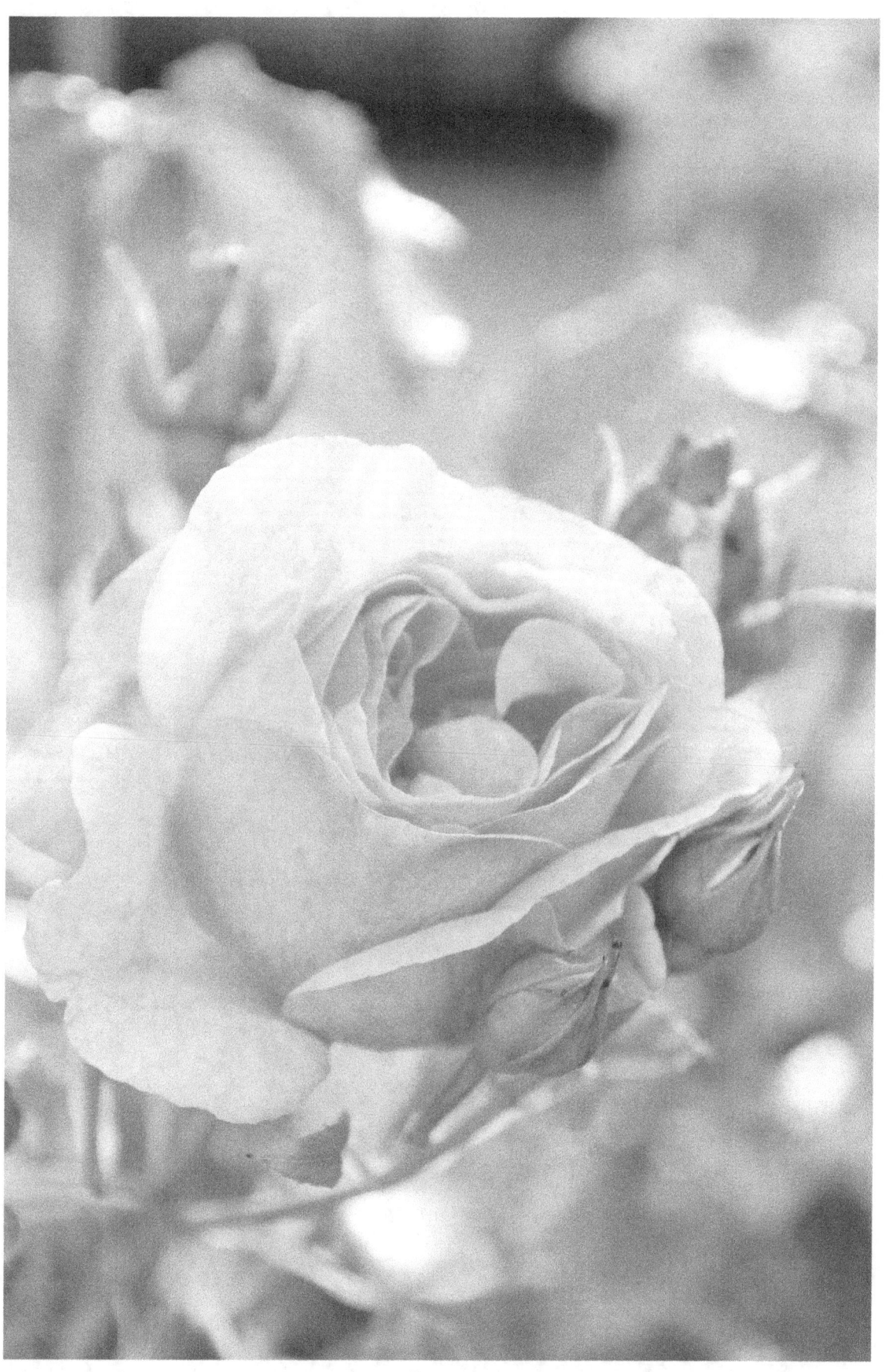

"A single rose can be my garden... a single friend, my world."
~ Leo Buscaglia

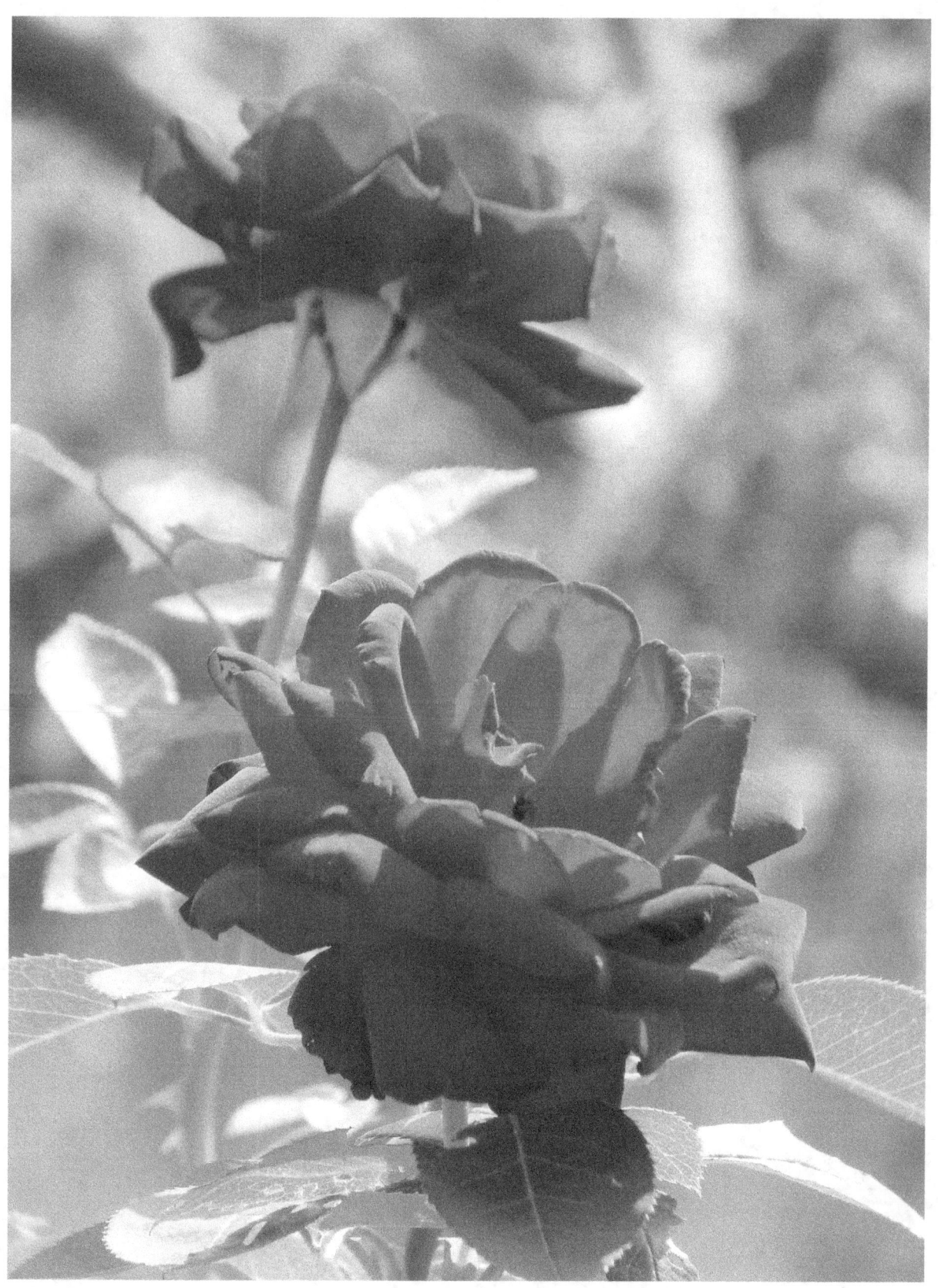

"How does it happen that birds sing, that snow melts, that the rose unfolds, that the dawn whitens behind the stark shapes of trees on the quivering summit of the hill? A kiss, and all was said."
~ Victor Hugo

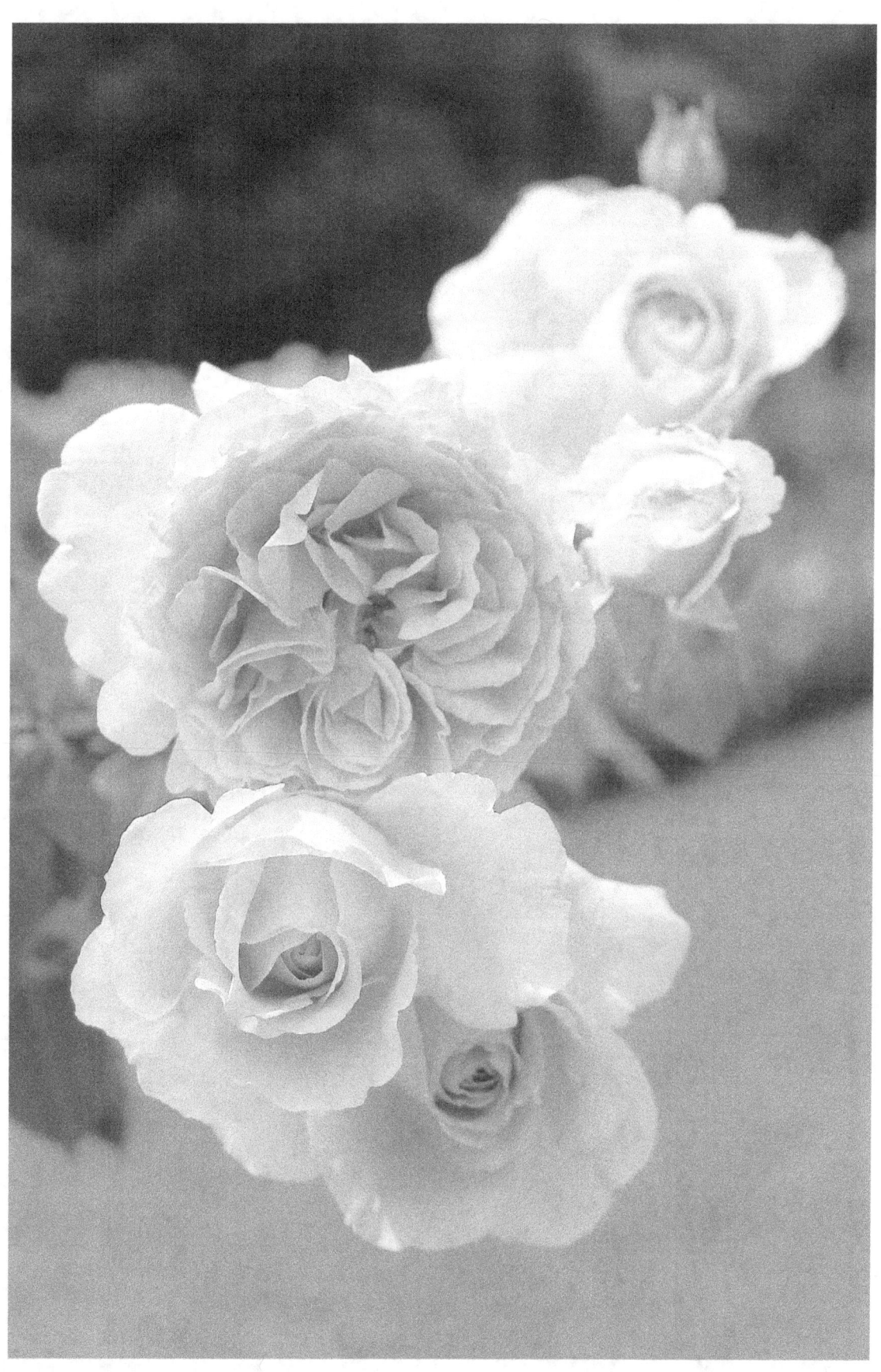

"There is nothing more difficult for a truly creative painter than to paint a rose, because before he can do so he has first to forget all the roses that were ever painted."
~ Henri Matisse

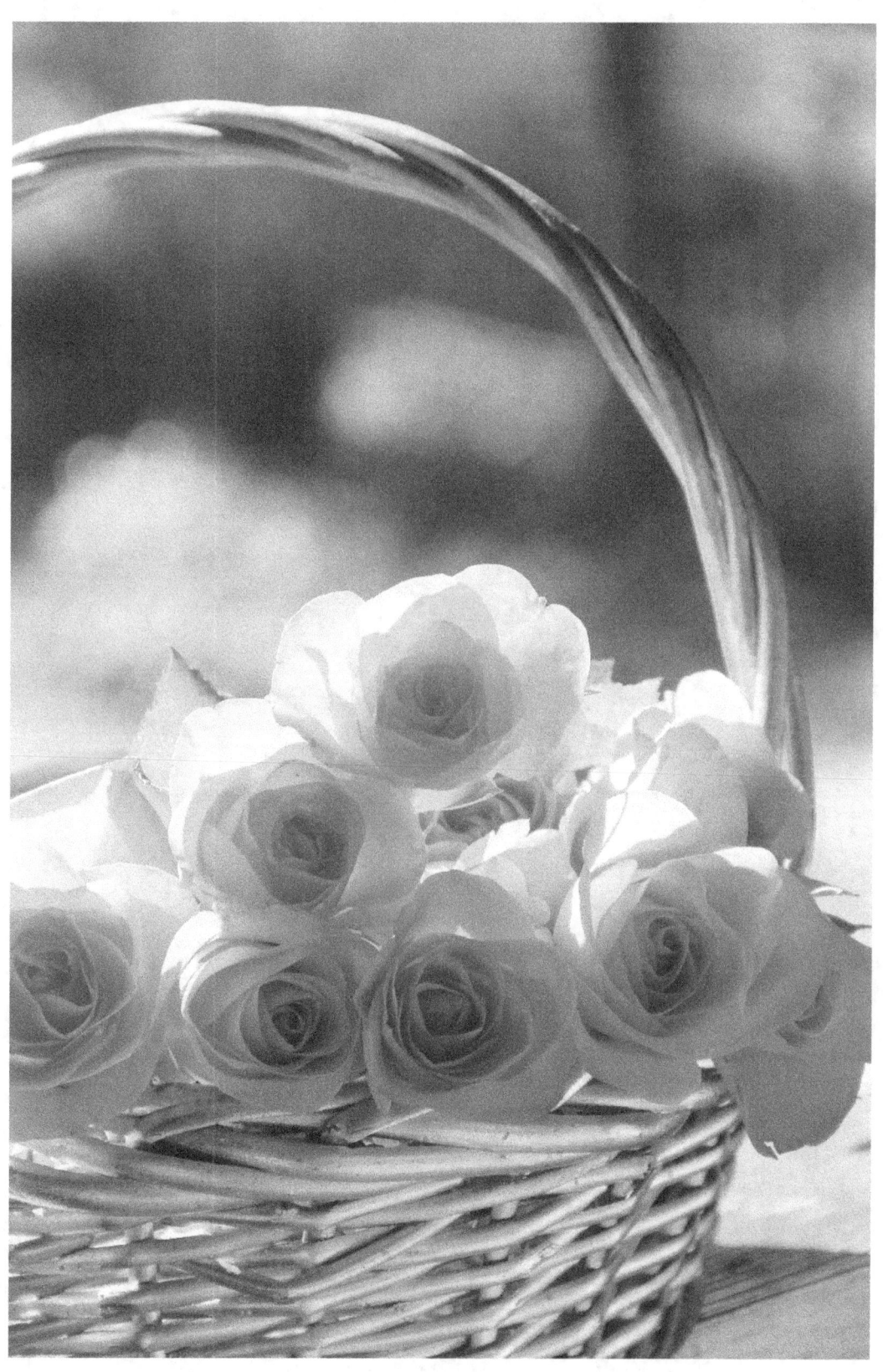

"*A basket full of roses brings with a peck full of fragrant memories.*"
~ Amish Proverb

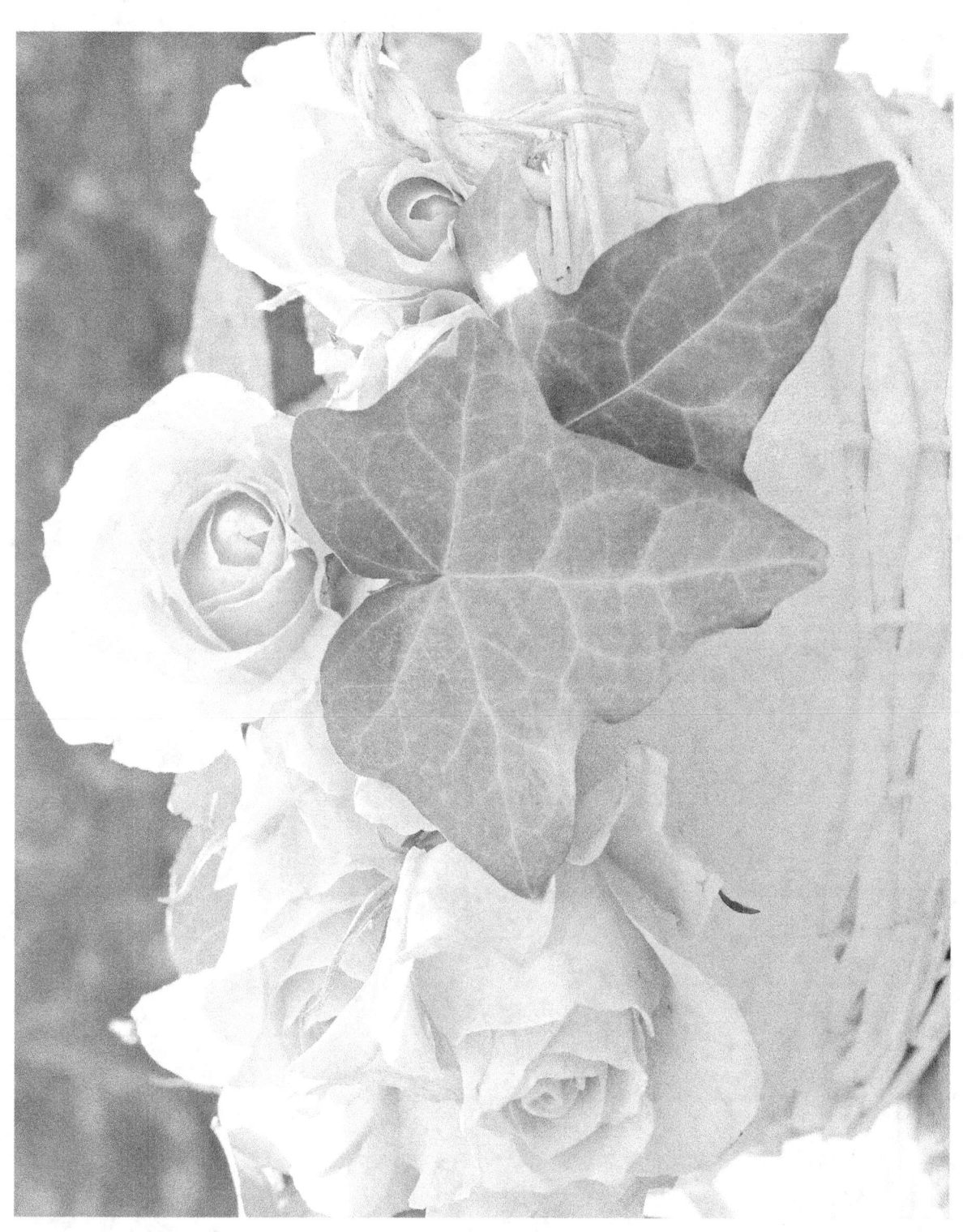

www.ingramcontent.com/pod-product-compliance
Lightning Source LLC
Chambersburg PA
CBHW081121240526
45470CB00019B/2837